REJECTED
But Not by
GOD

BONNIE DAVIS

WESTBOW
PRESS®
A DIVISION OF THOMAS NELSON
& ZONDERVAN

WestBow Press books may be ordered through booksellers or by contacting:

WestBow Press
A Division of Thomas Nelson & Zondervan
1663 Liberty Drive
Bloomington, IN 47403
www.westbowpress.com
844-714-3454

Scripture taken from the King James Version of the Bible.

ISBN: 978-1-6642-6569-1 (sc)
ISBN: 978-1-6642-6568-4 (e)

Print information available on the last page.

WestBow Press rev. date: 05/17/2022

Contents

Acknowledgments

I sincerely thank all my family and friends who offered encouragement, help, love, and prayers in making this book possible.

Many collaborative hours of writing, editing, and design work contributed to the completion of this book. I express my deep appreciation.

God bless all of you for every effort and the time spent working on this book.

My love and prayers,

Bonnie Davis

Prologue

HERE I AM, LORD

I pulled my Datsun up to the curb across the street from the school bus garage just before seven on a clear January morning. I looked at the clock on the dashboard. I had ten minutes before my check-in time. I reached for my Bible on the seat next to me. As I opened it, the thought came to me: *Bonnie, I want you to write your life story in a book.* I wondered if this thought had come from my mind or if God was speaking to me, so I said, "God, if this is from You, show me in my Bible." Then I opened my Bible at random, and my eyes fell on these words in Jeremiah 30:1-2, "The word that came to Jeremiah from the LORD, saying, Thus speaketh the LORD God of Israel, saying, Write thee all the words that I have spoken unto thee in a book."

After reading these words, I knew this was from the Lord. Feeling inadequate, I said, "Lord, how can I do this? Where do I start?" I opened my Bible again and this time read Isaiah 41:14-15, "Fear not, thou worm Jacob, and ye men of Israel; I will help thee, saith the Lord, and thy redeemer, the Holy One of Israel. Behold, I will make thee a new sharp threshing instrument having teeth: thou shalt thresh the mountains, and beat them small, and thou shalt make the hills as chaff." I thought, *If God can take a worm and thresh a mountain, then, Lord, I am that worm, and my life is that mountain. Use me for your glory.* The thought came to me again. I knew it was from God. "Bonnie, if you will begin to write, I will help you, and I will work in your life." I knew God would never forsake me and would help me in writing my testimony in book form.

1

GOD BROUGHT ME
INTO THIS WORLD

My Mama grew up in Vancouver, Washington, the eldest of eight children. When she was twenty, she moved across the river to Portland, Oregon to work in a candy factory. Mama was very shy and petite, with a beautiful complexion. She had long black hair that she wore in a bun. Mama met my dad when he came to visit a family where she and her sister were living in a boarding house. He invited her to attend church with him. The first time she entered the building, she felt the Spirit of God and she loved it. She attended Sunday school as a child, but never had a born-again experience in her heart. At nine years old, she contracted pneumonia in both lungs and wasn't expected to live. Her mother prayed for her and the Lord healed her.

During my parents' first year of marriage, they moved to Monroe, Washington, to live with his parents. While they were there, people from the Apostolic Faith Church in Seattle held cottage meetings in his parents' home. During a meeting one Sunday, my dad prayed and got saved. Mama saw a change in him. He was happy and began treating her differently. He quit being short with her and talking down to her. Suddenly, he had a wonderful love for his wife. When Mama saw the change in him, she said, "I want what you have."

"Just pray and ask Jesus to come into your heart," he replied.

She did and had a beautiful experience of salvation. She was so filled with happiness and peace. Dad looked at her and said, "You look like a flower after a shower."

A blessed year followed for them. Mama often talked about it as the happiest year of her life—a year of unity and love in the Lord. They had precious times reading their Bible together, praying, and serving the Lord. Then they moved back to Portland and began attending a church of the same faith in the downtown area, on Burnside Street.

After a time, work and outside influences affected Dad and he stopped reading and praying with Mama. One night as they walked across the Burnside bridge to go to church, Dad said, "I guess I won't go to church with you tonight. I'm going uptown."

Mama looked at him and remarked, "Pretty soon you won't go at all." That is exactly what he did.

He stopped going to church, and quit reading his Bible and praying. Soon he had drifted far away from the Lord. It didn't take long before his actions affected our family. Nothing made him happy anymore. He became demanding and was determined to have his way. Everything we as children did irritated him. He developed a temper that was beyond words.

———❖———

My parents lost their first child shortly after she was born. Mama became sick while carrying her second child. She developed severe nerve spasms of the esophagus, causing her to choke on her food. She lost weight and barely weighed 100 pounds. When she couldn't keep anything down, she sucked on big hunks of chocolate. She carried her last two babies in this condition and almost died with each of them, but God sustained her and gave her the strength to deliver them. The two of us were born healthy and normal, which was a miracle. Mama often quoted Deuteronomy 8:3: "Man doth not live by bread only, but by every word that proceedeth out of the mouth of the Lord."

On the day I was born, June 2, 1935, a Sunday evening, Mama was alone in our big two-story house with her three children: Leonard, age twelve; Vollie, age six; and Lavelda, twenty-two months. Mama was very weak and sick. While still pregnant with me, she dedicated me to the Lord just as she had done with all her children. She believed that God knew me before I was born. She quoted the scripture in Jeremiah 1:5: "Before I formed thee in the belly I knew thee; and before thou earnest forth out of the womb I sanctified thee, and I ordained thee a prophet unto the nations." Psalms 139:16 says: "Thine eyes did see my substance, yet being unperfect; and in thy book all my members were written, which in continuance were fashioned, when as yet there was none of them."

She was all alone in the house when she delivered me. My dad was gone that night, off at a dance with another woman. I weighed just five pounds, a tiny thing. Mama sent my oldest brother, Leonard, to the neighbors to call a lady from our church for help.

Sister Samuels was a dedicated Christian and a wonderful nurse. Soon after she came, she took me in her arms and looked at me for a few minutes. Then she turned to my mother and said, "This is the child you have been waiting for. She will be a blessing to you."

I was more like my mother than any of her other three children. I was the one whom she could talk to and the one who took care of her at the end of her life. As a child, I had a tender conscience. I couldn't lie to Mama. If I did something wrong, all she had to do was say, "Bonnie," and immediately I felt sorry. She taught me from the Bible and how to pray. I prayed and knew that God answered prayer, although I didn't realize the beauties of the gospel until I was older.

Me at age four with my dog, Mickie

Mama came down with pneumonia several times while I was growing up. When I was about six years old, she had double pneumonia and was not expected to live. We called the church and asked the ministers to pray and anoint her with oil according to the instructions in James 5:14-15, which reads, "Is any sick among you? Let him call for the elders of the church; and let them pray over him, anointing him with oil in the name of the Lord: And the prayer of faith shall save the sick, and the Lord shall raise him up; and if he have committed sins, they shall be forgiven him." The Lord healed Mama. This made an impression on me at that young age. During this illness, while she was so sick, Mama prayed, "Lord, please let me live long enough to raise my children." God answered that prayer. She was almost seventy-three when she went to be with Jesus.

I was six years old in 1941. Dad bought a brand-new, four-door, blue Studebaker, but our family hardly ever got to ride in it. Dad always wore a blue, pin-striped suit when he went out at night. I remember lying in the big, white, wrought iron bed, looking in the oval mirror on the dresser against the wall, and seeing the reflection of the headlights as they left the driveway. I always asked Mama, "Where is Daddy going?" and she would say, "I don't know, Honey. Out to a dance, I guess."

Dad, Mama, me, Lavelda, and Vollie with the 1941 Studebaker

I could tell Mama was deeply hurt by what Dad was doing. Sometimes I would get up in the middle of the night and see Mama crying, praying, and asking Jesus to make the house payment so we wouldn't lose it. Other times, I found her asleep bent over the sewing machine, emotionally and physically exhausted, attempting to sew dresses for my sister and me.

I disliked seeing Dad come home at night because I knew what he would do. He had a terrible temper. He'd start swearing and switch us. Everything we as children did irritated him. We tried to stay out of his way, but he seemed to take pleasure in demanding our attention.

Sometimes he commanded us children to go into the backyard and cut limbs from the flowering quince bush. It had lots of stems and green leaves with dusters of pink flowers. He'd strip the sticks to make switches then ordered my sister and me into the bathroom, locking the door, and beating us until the branches broke. I remember jumping all over the bathroom begging for him to stop, but Dad was a big man, and Mama was just as much afraid of him and his anger as we were.

Mama would beg him to stop beating us. She'd cry out, "Lee, please don't do this!" He didn't stop his abuse on us. Mama was afraid she would lose her kids if she turned him into the authorities. I know it was Mama's prayers that spared us from any further hurt. My dog would get frantic, barking and running through the house trying to protect us. Even he knew to stay a distance away. I know it was Mama's prayers over us that kept us from serious injury.

I remember a time when Dad put me in the basement to punish me. I sat on the basement steps in the dark, crying.

I was too afraid to turn on the light. I knew if I did he'd switch me. I sat there wishing he would go away and never come back. These were times of insecurity and emptiness in our home. I felt lonely because I didn't have a dad who loved me. We all suffered because of his sinful actions.

Soon after that incident, Dad came home less and less. He moved downtown with another woman when I was eight years old and returned home only two or three times a month. He gave Mama little money to live on. She would pray for our shoes, clothes, and everything we needed. God supplied all of our needs. Before my brother, Vollie, left home at age 17 to join the Navy in 1946, he bought a cow so we could have milk and had it butchered. The meat lasted for five years and we stored it in public lockers. It never had freezer burn or went bad. God was so good to us.

Clockwise from left: Mama, Dad, Leonard, Vollie, me, and Lavelda

2

GOD ANSWERED
MAMA'S PRAYERS

Mama was an old-fashioned Christian who had faith in Jesus that would move mountains. She prayed about everything, and as I grew up I watched God answer her prayers. One of those prayers was answered while I was in kindergarten. During recess, I went outside with all the other children and began playing on the monkey bars. I was at the top, and some others were below me, when my foot slipped. As I opened my mouth to yell, my jaw came down on the bar, and my top teeth went right through my tongue. The principal called my brother, Vollie, who was in the sixth grade. Vollie put me on his back and ran all the way home. My oldest brother, Leonard, was home. He and Mama took me to the church office, where the ministers prayed for me. The bleeding stopped.

Then she took me to the doctor. He said, "I'm sorry, but we can't sew up her tongue. She has cut and severed all the main tendons. She'll have a lisp to her speech. She won't be able to form her words and will not be able to sing or whistle."

Thank the Lord! He healed my tongue. I still have the teeth marks to remind me of what God did. Before my healing, my mouth was sore and I could only chew small bits of food at a time. To this day, I form my words with precision without a lisp, sing high soprano, and whistle bird calls. God did a wonderful and complete work on my tongue. I'm sure this healing came in answer to our prayers, especially Mama's.

Another time, our next-door neighbor, Mr. Weins, burned the field behind our barn because it was overgrown with weeds, blackberry vines, and morning glory flowers. After he put the fire out, we children went to play ball there. I was barely six years old. Being the first one out on the field, I didn't know that the fire hadn't been completely put out. With bare feet, I stepped right onto the hot ashes. When I realized the coals were hot, I couldn't do anything but just stand there and cry. My feet were badly burned. My brother, Vollie, picked me up and carried me to the house. Both of my feet were covered with blisters. I could not wear shoes. For months, I had to crawl wherever I went. Today, I have no scars on either of my feet. They were totally healed and have never bothered me since.

———

During October and November of 1949, when I was fourteen and beginning eighth grade, Mama and I visited my brother Leonard and his family in California when he was in the Navy.

Leonard, my oldest brother, died in a plane crash while serving the Navy in 1957

One day I went with some other children to a public swimming pool to play in the water. Like many swimming pools, this one was shallow at one end and deep at the other end. Someone threw a ball that went into the deep end of the pool. I hurried after it even though I couldn't swim. I went down to the bottom and came up three times.

The fourth time I stayed down, a total calmness came over me. I kept my eyes wide open and could see others swimming above me. I wanted to be up there with them, but I couldn't move. Finally, someone saw me lying down there and called for the lifeguard. When he pulled me out, everyone thought I had drowned. But the Lord had His hand over me and helped the lifeguard revive me. Mama's prayers were with me that day, and I know God spared my life.

There is no question God answers prayers! One Christmas, Mama asked the Lord if He would supply toys for us children. My dad came home that Christmas Eve just to bring us a doll bed and a doll buggy. I can still remember that Christmas. The buggy was covered with brown leather. It had black rubber tires with silver hubcaps and a hood that folded up and down like the big buggies. We put our dolls in it and pushed them around the house. Sometimes we put the cat in and pushed him around, too. We had so much fun with that buggy and doll bed. I remember that as being my best Christmas. I was eight and my sister, Lavelda, was ten. What we didn't know was that those toys had belonged to the children of my dad's girlfriend. When he told Mama where they came from, she never said a word to us. She knew God had sent them as an answer to her prayer.

Another time, Mama asked the Lord if we could have a Christmas tree for Christmas. Shortly after that, a knock sounded at the door. There stood a man. Mama didn't know who he was, but we children went to school with his son and knew he lived around the corner from us.

"Would you like to have a Christmas tree?" he asked.

"Yes," Mama told him.

It was a beautiful Christmas tree. It even had handmade ornaments on it. Mama thanked the Lord because she knew God had sent it. God's goodness was showcased throughout my entire life.

3

CHILDHOOD MEMORIES

My memory of old fashioned church camp meetings began when I was four years old. The church services were held ten blocks from our home in a large, open-air tabernacle. It had a big, gold star on the front that blazed out the words, "Jesus, the Light of the World." Mama and us children would walk to the tabernacle. It is set on a campground several acres in size. Many tall fir trees grew on the campgrounds. It was peaceful to walk on the paths among those trees. Campers stayed in tents and at night they lit their tents with coal oil lamps.

The Apostolic Faith Church Tabernacle

The grounds in front of the tabernacle were landscaped with gorgeous flowers and had a big stone fountain. Among the other fish was a giant Koi fish (goldfish) about two feet long, named Goliath. Koi fish are known for their long life spans. Goliath was about thirty-five years old when he was given to the church, and he lived there about fifty more years. We children could hardly wait for services to close so we could run to the fountain and see Goliath. Excitedly, we called, "Goliath, come here!" Slowly, Goliath would glide toward us. As we bent over the edge of the fountain and wiggled our fingers in the water, he opened his mouth hoping for fish food. He even allowed himself to be spoon-fed.

Our church had a large orchestra and choir. The music was beautiful and I loved listening to it. Everyone sat on wooden, slatted benches. The tabernacle had sawdust on the dirt floors to keep the dust down. During the church services and prayer meetings afterward, I would sit on the ground and play in the sawdust.

One afternoon I was sitting on the floor beside Mama, filling her handkerchief with sawdust, when I heard the minister, Brother Frost, say, "Zacchaeus, come down out of that tree; I am going to your house today." This caught my attention, because I had heard about Zacchaeus in Sunday school. Pointing to the ceiling, Brother Frost said, "Can't you just see Zacchaeus up in that tree?"

I got up from the sawdust-covered ground, climbed onto Mama's lap, and looked up to where he was pointing. I looked, but couldn't see Zacchaeus. I asked, "Where is he? I can't see him." This experience was very real to me. I vividly remember looking for Zacchaeus. The Lord was able to get my attention even though I was only four years old.

Children's church services were held in the old wooden building behind the tabernacle. There was a youth orchestra and I loved listening to the children play their musical instruments

I lived just walking distance from the church. Mrs. Dallas was a sweet neighbor, who resided just down the road from us. She had a big cat, tons of flowers, and lots of windows in her house. One time she and I walked out to the front porch and, pointing to a vine growing on a trellis, she asked, "Bonnie, do you know what this vine is?"

"No," I replied.

"This is what they call the Passion Flower. It represents Jesus dying on the cross. The pointed leaf is the symbol of the spear, which pierced His side. The tendrils that coil around the trellis to hold the vine in place are the whips and cords they used to lash Jesus." The little, round flower had an outside circle of white, oval petals, and inside that, a circle of needle-like, blue-purple and white petals. "The white circle is the crown of thorns Jesus wore. The blue-purple petals represent the robe they put on Him. The three red dots on the pistil divisions are the nails they drove through His hands and feet." I never forgot what she said as I had heard that in Sunday school.

4

GOD GAVE ME A FRIEND AND COMPANION

When I was nine years old, my Uncle Orville moved from his farm in the country to the city. He had to find a new home for his two-year-old dog and wanted a place where he could run and play. We lived in the country, so my uncle brought Tippy to us. The Lord sent him at just the right time. My dad had recently left us. I was feeling the emptiness in our home, and the Lord knew I needed a friend. I was a good-natured child, but was lonely.

Tippy was a mild mannered, brown and white shepherd dog. On days when the kids at school made fun of me, calling me a dummy, I came home and sat on the top step of the front porch with Tippy. I put my arm around him and buried my head in his fur, and just cried. He sat motionless beside me and looked up into my face with his big brown eyes as though to say, "I know and I care." I told him all my fears, my hurts, and disappointments. He was my comfort, my friend, and my companion.

Me at age nine with Tippy

On summer mornings, before we went out to play, Tippy would lay beside me on the sun porch while Mama read the Bible to us children for our devotional time. The sun streamed through the small-paned windows. Afterward, Tippy and I went for walks together up the dusty road. In the evenings, Tippy played hide-and-seek with the other children and me in the front yard. We told Tippy to sit and stay in the front yard, then we hid in the many bushes around our house. Tippy stayed until he heard us call, "Come and find us!" Then he didn't quit until he had found every one of us. We had great fun with him.

After we had Tippy for about two years, he came in

one evening dripping wet from the rain. I dried him off, but he started sneezing and coughing. There were big clots of mucus coming from his nose. Over the next few days, he lost his appetite and became listless. He had always run to the door to meet me as I came home from school each day, but now he lay on the floor not even wanting to play.

Mama didn't have money to take him to a veterinarian, so she went to the old Owl Drug Store downtown and told the pharmacist how Tippy was behaving. He vocalized, "Your dog has a distemper and needs to go to the veterinarian." The pharmacist didn't have anything that could help except a little bottle of oil. It wasn't medicine.

Mama came home and told me that Tippy had distemper (like phenomena in a person). "Let's pray. I believe that if we pray, God will heal our dog," she said.

There was nothing we could do but pray. Tippy was lying on the carpet. I covered him with a big, heavy towel and lay down beside him. I placed a church paper on him, because I knew that the ministers from our church had prayed over them. Mama put the papers on us when we were sick and we got better. I prayed it would work on Tippy. Then I laid my head next to his head and cried, begging God not to let my dog die.

I arrived home from school every day and took care of Tippy, keeping him warm and covered up. I would lie next to him, wiping the mucus from his nose when he sneezed and praying for Jesus to heal him. He was deathly ill for a while; not eating, lying listlessly on the carpet, and coughing so deeply that his stomach heaved. Then one day, I came home from school and Tippy was up eating. God had healed him completely! Tippy lived to be eleven years old.

Me at age 16 with Tippy

Another miracle took place during this time. God kept my dad away from the house the whole time Tippy was sick. If he'd seen Tippy lying on the floor sick, he would have had him put to sleep. He didn't want any animals in our home and expected the house to be kept immaculate all the time, even though he didn't live there.

Dad disliked Tippy. He would get mad and kick him. One time, Dad brought a little white poodle home and said, "Now get rid of that big dog." I was not about to get rid of Tippy. Dad didn't realize or care how much I needed and loved my dog. My sister and I took the little white poodle to our neighbor's house. They thought the dog was cute, so we sold it to them for five dollars and hurried home, excited and pleased with the money. I'm sure God provided even those five dollars for us.

5

GOD HELPED ME THROUGH SCHOOL

Every morning before I left for school; Mama sat on the living room couch with the Bible open on her lap. My sister and I would sit on the floor in front of her, while she braided our hair and read the Bible to us. I started school at age five, in 1940, with Miss Kane as my kindergarten teacher. It was a time of playing with toys, which I never had at home. We ran through the classroom, laughed, and had so much fun. Miss Kane was such a friendly teacher.

Then I went into first grade with Miss Brown. She was kind and patient with me, always speaking in a soft, sweet voice. She read to us often and I really liked her.

In the second grade, I went into Miss Sandstead's class. What a different lady Miss Sandstead was! She wore bright orange lipstick and lots of white powder on her face. She didn't want to touch anything with her hands for fear of germs, so she always carried a pencil with her. Whenever she

wanted one of us students to do something for her, she used the eraser end of the pencil to point at the thing she wanted us to touch. She would have us open and close doors, pull down blinds, and write on the blackboard.

Miss Sandstead spoke sharply in precise sentences. I really didn't know what to think of her because I had never come across anyone like her. She'd look at me and say, "Now, you can do this reading lesson if you really want to." I wanted to believe I could. I tried hard, but I still couldn't make sense of the letters on the page. For a while, a lady came to my classroom and took me down the hall to a small room, where there was a little table with two child-sized chairs. She sat on one side of the table and I sat on the other. She read to me from the book about Dick and Jane and their dog Spot, "See Spot. See Spot run. See Jane. See Jane run." Then she turned the book around toward me and said, "Now you read it."

I tried, but all the words ran together. I could see the pictures and knew what they were doing, but the words just didn't make sense. The woman persisted, but I couldn't decipher the words. One day she took me back to my homeroom class and mentioned to Miss Sandstead, "It's no use; she just can't read."

Miss Sandstead agreed, "It's not worth trying anymore."

From that day on, no one ever gave me extra help.

After that, I began to feel the insecurity of not fitting in. The other children saw me sitting in class, unable to do my lessons, and they looked at me as though something was wrong. I would see teachers talking together and looking at me, shaking their heads since they didn't know what to do with me. The children began to make fun of me, calling me,

"Dummy." I'd ask myself, "Am I really that dumb? What is wrong with me that I can't learn like the other children? I knew the alphabet, so why couldn't I learn to read?"

My teachers and I didn't know at the time that I had a reading disability called dyslexia. I'd sit in class and stare at the clock on the wall, studying the roman numerals. I could count the I, the II, and the III on it, but what did the rest of them mean? How could they make a 4 out of IV?

In many of my classes, I sat and daydreamed. I'd look out the window, ask to go to the restroom, get a drink; anything to get out of the classroom. I could hardly wait for the 3:30 p.m. bell to ring so I could go home.

I didn't have many friends at school. On Valentine's Day, I would only have a few cards in my box. One spring, Miss Sandstead's class put on a play. I wanted so much to be part of the class—to be part of a group. Miss Sandstead asked me if I wanted to be an iris flower. I remember the flowers were made of two-toned purple crepe paper. How good I felt about being chosen for something!

In the third grade, Miss Sandstead passed me on to Mrs. Long, not knowing what else to do with me. I tried so hard to read, especially when Vollie had a paper route. I often sat on the living room floor and helped him roll his papers before stuffing them in the canvas newspaper bag he would sling over his bicycle handlebars. I looked at the papers and wondered what the characters were saying to each other. I wanted to know so badly. I would ask Vollie to read them to me, but he was too busy.

In the fourth grade, I was sent from public school to a different school that had a special education program. I had an excellent teacher, Miss Chapman, who taught my small class of six. She was sweet and good to our small group. She tried to work with us, reading aloud to us most of the time however, my reading didn't improve.

Without any solutions, they sent me right back into a regular classroom. I didn't know what the other children were doing in any of the subjects. Suffering from the teasing and taunting they gave me, I dreaded getting up in the morning. I ached inside, knowing what I'd have to endure throughout the day. Some mornings, I woke up with a stomach ache and asked if I could stay home—especially on testing days. I understood what was being taught by the teachers if they verbally or visually communicated the lesson, but I couldn't answer textbook or test questions because of my inability to read.

At home, I felt safe and comfortable. I'd sit in the living room in the big, high-backed wooden rocking chair by the warm furnace listening to my favorite radio programs. Mama would be ironing, in the kitchen cooking, or in the basement doing the washing in our old wringer washer. It was a relief to stay home and not face all the teasing at school. Home was my safe place.

I remember one time the teacher wrote something on the blackboard and asked me to come up to the board. I went, but I didn't understand what she wanted. I stood there, not knowing what to do. Embarrassed, my mind went blank. I stood there and laughed to try to cover up the shame I felt. Through several school years, I tried to laugh things off because I hurt inside. I didn't know how to handle my pain.

My fifth-grade teacher, Miss Greenman, was a short little lady. She had a brown wig and always wore a green dress with a brown vest. Her voice was curt and quick. I remember her saying, "If you don't listen to me, this is what you will get." Then she would walk to the blackboard and drag her long fingernails down it until she got our full attention. Miss Greenman had a little mirror in the front of the room and another in the back of the room. She frequently went to one or the other, adjusting her wig. Miss Greenman would arrange the pupils' pictures and drawings above the blackboard around the room. I longed for some of mine to be up there too, but never felt what I made was as good as the other students' pieces. I lacked self-confidence and self-esteem.

I made the best I could out of fifth grade. I was good at art, music, and enjoyed singing. I had a very high soprano voice and memorized songs from the radio. I was athletic as well. One time, a classmate wrote in my autograph book, "You're a dummy, but that doesn't include your tumbling (gymnastics ability)." I loved shop class and making projects out of wood. In shop class, I remember making a fish-shaped cutting board and a napkin holder with my initials on it.

During recess, my schoolmates and I would play softball. Even though I played well and had once hit a home run, I was always left standing until the teacher told someone to choose me. It was the same when we played Red Rover. It was another stab in my heart. I don't remember hearing compliments from any of my teachers or my dad. I knew Mama loved and cared about me. She tried to encourage me, but I never heard anybody say, "Bonnie, that's good!" or "You can do it!" in order to give me the confidence I needed. Year after year, self-pity overwhelmed me. I wondered, "Why did I have to be born this way?"

School continued to be a challenge for me. I went from fifth to Miss Chambers' sixth-grade class. She was friendly towards me. In seventh grade, I had Miss Olivia. She was French and had a strong accent. I enjoyed it when she talked about geography. In the front of the room, she had a big map that pulled down. It was interesting to hear about other countries, their people, and how they lived.

Mr. Sayler was my eighth-grade teacher. He sent me on to high school without passing me.

I really enjoyed high school. I felt more grown up there, and my classmates didn't pick on me. I didn't experience the ridicule, disappointments, hurts, and crying I had suffered in grade school. There was one girl who took pity on me and tried to help me through my classes. I realized, though, that her way of helping me was cheating, and my conscience wouldn't let me do that.

Mrs. Swanson, my home economics teacher, was good to me. I couldn't read the recipes, and some of the girls helped by telling me the list of ingredients. Because of their kindness, I started believing in myself. I longed for an outstanding grade in class. I wanted someone to say, "You made it! You've got something good inside of you."

In home economics, each student was asked to clean a stove. I scrubbed and scrubbed my stove oven in the classroom. Mrs. Swanson was impressed and told the class I had the cleanest stove in the classroom. I'd been recognized for something and ended up getting the best grade I had ever received. I felt I had accomplished something, even if it wasn't much.

In high school English I couldn't read. Though determined, I continued struggling in school. Teachers handed me from class to class. Science, math, and other subjects were way over my head. I was there eight months when the dean called my mother and voiced, "Your daughter is unable to do the schoolwork, and we don't know what to do with her. We don't have any special education classes to put her in. We suggest you take her out of school."

I left school in 1952 feeling rejected and lonely, just as I had felt in grade school. My poor mother suffered too. She wanted me to finish high school. I thought, *Why don't they understand me? Why can't anyone help me?*

6

GOD GAVE ME PEACE
AND HAPPINESS DURING
A FAILED MARRIAGE

I met my husband, Milton, when I was seventeen years old.
My sister had begun working as an usherette in a local
movie theater. When I saw that she made more money at the
theater than I could at babysitting and since the job didn't
require reading ability, I quit babysitting and went to work
in another theater. Mama didn't want me to get a job there,
but I didn't listen.

On Thursday evening in January 1953, after working
at the theater for several months, my girlfriend asked if I
wanted to join her to meet her boyfriend. Because I didn't
have anything else to do, I agreed. They were planning to
meet up with her boyfriend's buddy, Milton. We drove to
the training school where Milton was taking a sheet metal
class two nights a week. The four of us got into Milton's

car, a brand-new Ford, which impressed me. We drove to the Pittock Mansion, a local historical location. Milton drove right up onto the lawn, and the three of them began drinking. I didn't drink, but luckily we were there for a short time before Milton drove me home.

About a week later, Milton showed up at the theater where I was working and asked if I wanted to go out. Unaware that Milton had approached me, a boy I knew asked if I needed a ride home. Milton spoke up immediately, insisting he would take me home. I didn't have a good feeling about it since Milton was drinking the first time I met him. However, at this time the other boy had left and I didn't have anyone to go out with, so I accepted.

Milton made me feel special that day. He took me out to eat and for Valentine's Day, he bought me a box of chocolates. Another time, he brought me to a concert. Our relationship grew. When I was sick he'd bring me roses. I wasn't used to having anyone be so good to me. I liked him because he had a soft voice, unlike my dad. I thought because of his acts of kindness, he loved me.

After dating for three months, Milton drove me up to a secluded place. We sat in the car and kissed. One thing led to another. I felt the situation was going too far, so I opened the door and left the vehicle. Milton saw what I was doing, got outside the car, and persuaded me to get back in. When I returned, he overpowered my resistance and took advantage of me. It happened so fast.

I asked Milton to take me home and never said a word to anyone. The feeling of humiliation and confusion flooded my mind. I couldn't believe he would do this to me. Did

Milton do this because he loved and desired me? Was this love?

Because Milton had taken advantage of me, I felt I needed to marry him. I also thought nice things would make me happy. Milton had a new car and a good job. He came from a loving family. His parents had a nice home and were good people. They treated me well, and I got along fine with them.

Milton didn't want to marry me, though, because he had just come back from Korea five months earlier. He had a girlfriend there he wanted to marry. He wanted to bring her home, but his parents said no.

I never told Mama what Milton had done, but she could see that our relationship was not in God's will. She begged me not to marry him. The young man was seven and a half years older than I and came from a background completely different from mine. I never talked to God about it. I just thought that if I ever wanted to go back to God and be a Christian, Milton would go with me.

If I had only listened to Mama, prayed, and asked God whom I should marry! I would have saved myself a lot of heartache and many unhappy years.

During this time, I turned away from God and the training I had as a child. Milton and I knew each other only four months before I talked him into marrying me. We had a lovely church wedding on June 4, 1953, two days after my eighteenth birthday. *Now,* I thought, *my life will be happy.*

Milton and I on our wedding day in 1953

As we left on our honeymoon, I felt I had married a stranger. I carried a guilty secret. I never told the man I married that I couldn't read. In fact, I told him very little about my personal life, and I didn't know much about his. He was smart and had a good education. I felt if I told him I couldn't read or cook, he might not have married me.

There was no love in our marriage. Milton wouldn't call me by my name, he never paid me a compliment, and he never said, "I love you." In fact, he told me he didn't love me. I don't think I really loved him, either, because I didn't understand what real love was.

About a week after our wedding day, my husband discovered I couldn't read when I wasn't able to read a cookbook. I explained that I could make out some of the words, but couldn't sit down and read a book or newspaper. When he heard this, he was furious. "Don't tell me I've married a dumb woman!" he remarked, before leaving the house angry.

After Milton discovered I couldn't read, everything I did upset him. He became moody and sometimes wouldn't speak at all, except to argue. Two evenings a week he went to class to learn about sheet metal. After class, instead of coming home, he stayed out drinking until early in the morning. I begged him to stay home with me.

I asked Milton one time how he started drinking in the first place. He said he was just trying to fit in with the other boys in high school when he was sixteen. As an adult, Milton was a quiet man who had trouble expressing himself. He was uncomfortable around other people. Alcohol helped him to be more talkative.

I lived in a house filled with anger. Milton made all the decisions and never asked my opinion about anything he purchased. He bought a car and told me, "You don't touch it. It's mine." He'd persistently remind me that everything was his. For me, loneliness set in as I realized the big mistake I had made. I cried often. Before we had been married one full month, Milton said, "I don't love you, and I don't want to stay married to you."

I responded with conviction, "I won't divorce you because I made a vow before God to stay married to you until death, and I can't break it." That didn't sit well with him. Our relationship continued to feel divided.

One day I asked, "Milton, why did you marry me in the first place?"

"You were fun to be with, and all my friends liked you. You were attractive and I thought this was what I wanted, but I was wrong." I should have known he felt this way because he wasn't friendly with my family or any of my friends.

Three months after we were married, I became pregnant. Milton didn't want children and didn't want to be tied down. "I want this baby," I told him. The following day after he left for work, I went into my bedroom, dropped to my knees, and asked Jesus if He would give me a normal, healthy baby. I was worried the stress I was under could harm my baby. I was not a Christian at the time, but I did know how to pray. I'm thankful I had a Christain mother who taught me how to pray when I needed it the most.

The Lord answered my prayers. In June 1954, our son, Michael, was born—a normal and healthy baby. When Michael arrived, Milton loved his son and was very good to him.

My son, Michael

Though I had a happy, smiling baby, I cried most of the time. When Milton was at home in the evenings, he watched TV. I tried to engage him in conversation, but he only answered with a few words or not at all. His lack of attention or support hurt me. This attitude brought back terrible, unhappy memories of my childhood and the problems I had with my father.

One evening when Milton was out drinking, I felt very lonely and unhappy. I went into the bathroom thinking, *Life isn't worth living. Why don't you end it all?* My mind was dangerously mixed up, and I felt my life wasn't worth anything. As I stood there crying and looking into the mirror, God spoke to my heart, "Bonnie, your life is not yours to take. You know better than that. You know you'll go to hell. Who is going to raise that baby in the other room?"

My son was only seven and a half months old at the

time. I knew I had been wrong to consider taking my own life. I dropped to my knees there in the bathroom and cried out, "Oh, God, please help me!" I felt a calmness come over me.

My mother called shortly after that incident and asked, "Bonnie, won't you come to church with me?" I didn't go right away because I was afraid to give my heart to the Lord. I thought that as bad as things were at home, if I became a Christian things would be worse. On the other hand, I couldn't stand the way I was living and was very unhappy.

I decided my situation couldn't get any worse. I went to church with my mother on a Sunday evening. At the end of the sermon, the minister said, "Is there anyone here who would like to ask Jesus into their heart?" I raised my hand. He gave the invitation to come to the altar to pray. I literally ran to the altar and fell on my knees. I wanted peace and happiness more than anything else in this world. I asked Jesus to come into my heart. He didn't ignore me. He gave me peace and joy I never knew existed in this world! It was as if God's Spirit came down and calmed a raging ocean inside of me. All the bitterness I held in my heart for my dad and my husband were gone. I felt so peaceful and happy.

At home, I no longer showed disrespect to Milton. I responded to him with a soft tone. I didn't talk back or do anything that would cause him to argue. When Milton found out I was a Christian, he was angry, but the Lord helped me. I continued to live the way I felt Christ wanted me to live, and I tried to teach our son according to the Word of God.

When Michael was two years old, I bought a Bible storybook. He liked to look at the pictures. Since I couldn't read, I'd make up the stories I remembered from my childhood. His favorite story was 'Daniel in the lion's den.' When he learned to read, he would read the Bible to me. I prayed and asked God to please let my little boy give his heart to Him. I did not realize that the prayer I prayed was dedicating my child to God. All through his early years, I made sure he and I went to church.

Mama, Michael, and I on the church campgrounds, 1961

Shortly after, I got a job and bought a 1947 Chrysler for $95. I received my driver's license but didn't tell Milton about the purchase I had made. I'd park the car around the corner from our house and use it only to get groceries and attend church. One day I forgot and drove in front of our house with Michael in the backseat. Milton saw me. He was standing on the front lawn with rage on his face. "Sell that piece of junk," he demanded. There was no convincing him otherwise. So, I did exactly that and sold it for $100.

Milton, Michael (4 yr. old), and I, 1958

When Michael began kindergarten, Milton brought home a Vespa scooter. "You can use it to take Michael to school," he said. I wasn't allowed to drive it anywhere else. Although Milton and I's relationship grew further apart, I began to observe the way he loved on Michael. He'd bring him gifts such as tricycles as well as other various toys. "Michael, I have something for you," he'd say with a grin on his face. I watched as Michael enjoyed these kind gestures. I felt left out and was unable to give my son the same type of gifts.

One day Milton told me, "I'm leaving." It was Memorial Day of 1961, two days before my twenty-sixth birthday and nearly eight and a half years of marriage. I had no money and a six-year-old boy to feed. I didn't have any job skills, and I couldn't read a job application. What was I going to do to support us? I couldn't function. I curled into a ball and cried, which happened continuously.

My sweet mother helped a lot. I stayed with her and sometimes she stayed at my house to take care of Michael and I. These were tough times. Seven months later, on January 13, 1962, I had a nervous breakdown and was rushed into the hospital. They kept me there for three days before I was released. When I got out of the hospital, a woman from my church gave me three dollars. It bought us bread and milk. My mother helped provide us with food while Milton made the house payments so the bank wouldn't repossess it. He also paid the utility payments for Michael's sake. We at least had a roof over our heads.

Throughout this difficult season, I continued being in a posture of thankfulness. I'm grateful I had God and my Bible. I could hardly read, but did my best to make out the words. "Lord," I prayed, "will you please give me a passage that I can read, and show me something that I need to hear right now? I'm so alone. I don't know which way to turn or what to do." I opened the Bible to Psalm 37:25 and read, "I have been young, and now am old: yet have I not seen the righteous forsaken, nor his seed begging bread." As I read, the thought came to me, *I can read!* When I told my mother, she responded, "Bonnie, with the Lord's help you're going to learn to read." Later, He helped me do just that.

I went to court for the divorce on February 26, 1962. While we were in the courtroom, I prayed for God to show Milton that the gospel (of Jesus Christ) is real.

7

GOD TAUGHT ME
TO READ

After Milton left me, I stayed with my mother and she became my support. I knew she had a small income, and I didn't want to make her burden heavier. I needed a job.

"I don't have my health. I don't have an education. What can I do?" I cried to my mother.

"Bonnie, do you think God has forsaken you?" she asked.

"No," I answered with confidence.

"We're going to pray," was her answer to everything. That is when my healing began.

One night as we walked past a bank building in downtown Portland, a lady inside doing janitorial work caught our attention. Mama said, "Look, Bonnie, at how peaceful and quiet it is in that building. That kind of work would be good for your nerves." At that time, I couldn't stand the noise of a door closing or the clapping of hands.

Any sound caused me to shake all over and cry. I applied for the job and began to do janitorial work in that very same building. I continued to work there for the next six years. I worked nights while Mama babysat Michael, who was six years old. During that time, God completely healed my nerves.

It was also during this time that God taught me to read. "We are going to start with the Bible," Mama said.

"Oh, Mom, that's the hardest book in the world to read," I responded.

"That's all right. With God's help, we are going to teach you to read."

Mama didn't have much education. Having been sickly as a girl, she never got past the fifth grade in school, but was determined to help me. Before starting my reading lesson, she prayed for God to help us. Then she began reading the Bible to me, pointing to each word as she read.

She started with one word, broke it down into parts, and repeated the sound of each section several times. Seeing the word in individual parts made the process easier because I had trouble distinguishing one letter from another and one word from another. The words *through* and *though* looked the same to me. Sounding the words out was another way she taught me.

Next, Mama showed me the entire word. I memorized how it looked and its spelling. We started with small words like *it* because bigger words had too many parts all bunched together. Until I became comfortable in breaking down the words, trying to learn larger ones was too overwhelming.

Mama would tell me the meaning and how it could be used in a story. To remember a word, I had to associate what that word looked like, what it meant, and in what context I heard it used. For example, to remember the word *hear* I had to picture the word in my mind and associate it with someone saying, "I hear you." To remember the word *here*, I had to picture it in my mind and associate it with someone saying "Come here."

Names didn't have a meaning or a context. When I was introduced to someone, I remembered their name by associating it with someone else I knew by the same name. Learning to read was altogether a slow process because I could only concentrate on one word at a time. For each word, I had to recognize its separate sounds, memorize what it looked like, learn its meaning, and remember what context I had heard it used. We continued day after day, and I soon realized God was teaching me to read.

In all, the Lord showed my mother a distinct method on how to teach me. This included using slashes to divide words (ex. re/turn/ing). Little did I know that today, professionals use the same method for those struggling to read. There is no question that God is the creator of all things. Today I love to read, and I'm able to say, "I can do all things through Christ which strengtheneth me" (Philippians 3:14).

8

WHAT IS DYSLEXIA?

I learned that the reason I couldn't read like other children was not because I was dumb, but because I have dyslexia. Dyslexia is a language-based learning disability that affects about ten percent of the population with symptoms such as: the inability to recognize words and letters on a printed page; spelling, writing, and speaking difficulties, and a reading ability well below the expected age-appropriate level. Brain images taken of people while they are reading show the dyslexic reader's brain fails to use all of the same regions of the brain the non-dyslexic reader uses. Dyslexia manifests itself differently in different people. Some people see words from right to left instead of left to right. Others see words upside down or grouped together. Some people see the words swimming around the page or even swimming off the page. If left undiagnosed, dyslexia can lead to low self-esteem and behavioral problems. However, it does not affect a person's intelligence. Studies indicate that Thomas

Edison, Albert Einstein, Winston Churchill, and George Washington all may have had dyslexia. If testing is done, an appropriate learning strategy can be developed, and the dyslexic person can learn to read.

People with dyslexia feel stupid, ashamed, insecure, low self-worth, rejected, and avoid taking part in activities that require reading or spelling. Spelling is difficult because they are very slow to process their words. Under pressure, they are unable to think or concentrate. They get frustrated, cry, become angry, or freeze. When people speak rapidly, they may not understand all the words that are said or the sounds of the words. When writing, they are prone to write some letters backwards, such as b or d, p or q. It is very difficult to make decisions if there are two or three choices. Some need a quiet place with no distractions when testing.

There are many theories about what causes dyslexia. Researchers believe the brain disorder begins to take shape before birth, perhaps during the second trimester of pregnancy, while the cortex of the brain is being formed. The disability tends to run in families, so it appears there is a genetic link. More males than females have dyslexia, so it is likely testosterone plays a part as well.

9

GOD HELPED ME
FIND A JOB

I worked nights for six years. Though my mother had been taking good care of Michael while I worked, I knew it was time for me to be at home with him. I started praying about the situation because I still had to work to support us.

God heard my prayers. One night as I rode home on the city bus after work, the bus driver asked me, "Why are you working nights, as young as you are?" I didn't want to tell him, and he asked me further, "Why don't you drive a school bus during the day like I do?"

My immediate reaction was, "Oh no, I could never do something like that." I had no self-confidence.

"You don't know until you try," he responded. I knew this was true. He encouraged me to talk to the man he drove for—a man named Jack, who owned a school bus company. I loved to drive and I loved children.

God's timing was perfect. The problem with my nerves

was healed. I told my mom what the bus driver had said, and she replied, "Bonnie, let's pray about it." I began to pray earnestly about driving a school bus. Then I went to see this man, Jack. He asked if I had a chauffeur's license. I didn't. He suggested I get one and come back.

I began to pray about taking the chauffeur's driving test. I studied and studied the manual and asked the Lord to help me. I told God, "If this is Your will, if this is the job You want me to have, then please see that I pass the test." I got a ninety-three on that test! It was the first passing grade I had ever received. I was overwhelmed with happiness. I thought, *Surely God is in this.*

I went back to Jack and showed him my chauffeur's license. "Can I drive a bus now?" I asked.

"Let's go out and get into one," he said.

All my fears dissipated as I pulled myself up into the step-well and looked around. I sat down in the driver's seat and thought to myself, *I'm home.* I felt like I belonged there. That's when I knew God was in all of this and He had a plan for my life.

Jack had me take the bus out. As we went, he told me how to drive it. I already knew how to drive a stick shift, but this bus was so big and I was only 5'1". I could hardly see over the steering wheel. Jack showed me when to shift, how to turn corners, and how to use my mirrors. After about four blocks I remarked, "This bus is so long."

"Yes, but you don't have to worry," Jack assured me. "The back end will follow the front." We laughed and then he told me to drive him back to the garage.

When we got back, Jack told me to take the bus out and practice by myself. "All by myself?" I asked. "Do you have faith in me that I can take care of this bus all by myself after only four blocks?"

"I believe you are going to make a good driver," Jack stated.

This gave me confidence. *Someone believes in me*, I thought. I took the bus out by myself on a country road. When I looked for a place to turn around, I couldn't find any. I started praying, "Oh Lord, help me. He didn't tell me how to turn this bus around or how to back it up." Jack hadn't even told me how to read the gauges on the dashboard. I saw a big cow pasture and drove the bus into it to turn around. When I got back to the garage, I asked Jack if I could come and practice driving his buses. He said I could, so every day for two weeks I went back and practiced driving.

During the summer, I kept praying about the job and continued working long nights at the bank as a janitor. I planned to call Jack for a job once Clackamas schools started up again. He had not informed me there were no openings for drivers.

That fall, as school time approached, I called Jack. "I'm sorry Bonnie, I have no openings," he stated. "I suggest you call Multnomah County School District 1. They just bought some new buses. Go there and ask for Ben."

Little did I know that this would be an answer to prayer. Jack was just a contractor for the Clackamas school district. This meant he didn't have any retirement plan. When Jack suggested I go to Multnomah County, I discovered that they did have a retirement program in place.

Once I entered the school bus garage, I introduced myself to Ben and asked for a job. Ben didn't question whether I had a high school diploma. He handed me an application. I filled out the application right there and gave it back. "Do you have driving experience?" he asked. I had two weeks of experience, so I said yes, and he hired me.

Ben rode along with me as we drove the bus route. I wasn't used to the West Hills of Portland, let alone driving a bus up those winding, narrow roads. I could look down over the tops of the fir trees into the canyon below. The roads had no curbs or sidewalks.

"This scares me," I told him.

"Well," he replied, "maybe you don't want to drive up here."

"Oh, yes, I do," I answered. I was sure the Lord had this planned for me.

When I started there in the fall of 1967, we had only four buses. We parked them at Sylvan School under a carport. I had a wonderful bus route with a very patient boss. One time I put a dent in the side of the bus. Instead of counting it against my record, Ben said it was no problem and he fixed it.

I loved the students who rode with me and enjoyed driving through the hills. I had three separate runs each morning and each afternoon, picking up over 150 children in all. Besides these, I had a kindergarten run at noon. I also did home economic and shop class runs. In the evenings, I sometimes took bands and choirs to hospitals and other places to sing.

In the spring and fall, I had outdoor school runs on the weekends. All this kept me very busy, gave me a job I loved, and allowed me to be home with my son when school was out.

10

GOD HEALED ME
OF CANCER

I had been driving the school bus for three years when my mother became ill with pneumonia. Infection set in, and she began to get very weak. She was bedridden for five months. We did not expect her to live. I came home between bus runs to take care of her. Often, I had to be up at night with her. This was never a burden, because I loved her. My son was in his mid-teens at the time. I was trying to meet his needs, along with all the other duties around the house, as well as my job. I knew that I was not well myself, but ignored my feelings.

One day Ben said to me, "Bonnie, you are not well."

"I'll be alright once my mother feels better and is on her feet again," I told him.

"No, there is something else wrong with you," he insisted. "I want you to go see the doctor."

I knew the law required public school bus drivers to

keep themselves physically fit. I understand it was Ben's business to keep an eye on the health of his drivers. Ben was right in noticing that I looked sick.

Springtime in 1970 had come, and my route in Portland's West Hills was scenic and beautiful. Everything seemed just right except for the way I felt. For weeks I had been feeling exceptionally tired. Sometimes I was so exhausted I wondered whether I would be able to finish my bus runs for the day. I thought maybe I was doing more than I could handle with three separate trips each morning and afternoon. The bus I drove was a big one, about thirty-five feet long, and I was a small woman. This was a challenging job for me.

After Ben spoke to me about seeing a doctor, physical symptoms began to appear that alarmed me. I started having pain in my back, my chest, and in my left arm to my elbow. I discovered a lump on my breast and another in my armpit. Both were very sore and tender. Then I began to suffer from severe pressure in my head. It felt like my head was in a vise that squeezed tighter and tighter. I soon realized something was seriously wrong. As a bus driver, I knew I needed to see a doctor.

The doctor wanted me to go to the hospital for a biopsy. I went for the biopsy on February 19, 1970. I knew of God's power to heal, so I began to pray and ask the Lord to show me what to do. When the doctor received the biopsy report, he told me that my body was full of a severe type of cancer. He wanted to perform an operation immediately in the area where the cancer had originated. I knew that one operation would not rid me of the cancer. I asked, "Doctor, if you do this, what about the cancer elsewhere in my body?" He seemed to have no answer.

I did not want the operation. I could not afford it financially or spiritually. I did not know whether it was God's will to heal me, but I knew He could. I felt I had to look to Him in faith for my healing. I said to the doctor, "I am sorry, but I do not feel led to have this operation. If it is God's will, I will live. If not, then it will be my time to go." He held out little hope for me without surgery and warned me not to wait more than two or three weeks.

After the tissue was cut into for the biopsy, the cancer spread like wildfire throughout my body. The pain grew more and more intense. I could hardly think straight at times. I grew weaker. It seemed like my life was ebbing away. The enemy of my soul kept telling me, "If you do not have that operation, you will die." The Lord spoke to my heart, saying, "Have faith! Keep holding on! Keep believing!" That is what I did. As I fought against the doubts and fears that came to me, the Lord strengthened my soul. He gave me more faith as my body grew weaker.

One day I was almost overcome with pain. I felt as though I was choking to death; I could hardly swallow. I cried out, "Lord, I don't want to die, but if it is Your will, heal me so I can take care of my family." The discouraging thought came to me, "You cannot live. You are full of cancer." I kept right on pleading for my life, making deeper consecrations to the Lord. Once again I prayed, "Oh, Lord, please heal me, for Your honor and glory."

As I prayed, I looked up into the sky and noticed a big, beautiful, white cloud that seemed to be coming toward me. It was as if the Lord was speaking to me right out of the cloud. "I am the Lord that healeth thee" (Exodus 15:26). I knew those words came from heaven above. I grabbed hold of that promise and held onto it as firmly as a drowning man holds a rescuer's rope.

I promised the Lord if He helped me, I would go to church and ask the ministers to pray for me as the Bible instructs us to do. I believed if I did this, I would be healed. That night, though in much pain and very weak, I went to church. After the service the ministers anointed my head with oil and prayed for me according to the instructions in James 5:14-15, and the Lord instantly healed me! Not only that, He blessed me in the most marvelous way. He gave me a glorious vision. It was the most beautiful experience I have ever had in my life. As I continued in prayer, I felt as though Jesus took me into His arms and carried me away in the spirit. Stretching before me for miles and miles in every direction, I saw vast fields of people. There were men, women, and children of all ages and races.

I did not understand the vision then, but I do now. The people I saw were lost and dying souls who needed to be told about Jesus. I was to tell them not only of God's power to heal, but also of what it means to be a born again Christian, to have a spiritual experience that takes a person out of sin and makes him a new creation in Christ Jesus.

When this vision of the fields of people passed from my view, I saw an hourglass. It appeared to be running out, and the Lord kept saying to me, "The time is very short." During this time of communing with my Lord, I was so engulfed in the Spirit that I did not realize where I was. When I opened my eyes and looked around, I realized I was in church. All around me were Christian friends who had seen me in my state of weakness and knew how I had suffered. Now, though, things were different. I felt new strength in my body as a warm sensation began at my feet and traveled to my head. The pain was gone! I felt my breasts, and the lumps were gone! I hadn't had any appetite for days and was very thin, but now I was hungry and wanted something to eat. Jesus had completely healed me! How I rejoiced in Him for what He had done!

The next day the cancer began passing from my body a little at a time and kept on doing so for several weeks. I began to feel stronger. I kept driving the school bus after my healing. When the time came for another physical checkup on June 6, four of the best specialists in the city carefully analyzed my case for a whole week and found no trace of cancer.

Today, many years later, I am still free of that disease. The Lord gave me a new start in life when He healed me. He also gave me a greater insight into the beauties of the gospel. I want to fulfill the commission He gave me.

For further information on my cancer story, write to the Apostolic Faith Church at the following address and ask for Tract 27 (Diagnosis Cancer):

Apostolic Faith Church
International Headquarters
5414 SE Duke
Portland, OR 97206
www.apostolicfaith.org

11

GOD PUT ME INTO
HIS HARVEST FIELD

My mother died in December 1970. Before she died, she prayed two prayers. She asked, "Lord, see that Bonnie doesn't need a babysitter and that she is well grounded spiritually." She died ten months after her prayers were answered. I was healed of cancer and didn't need help with Michael anymore as he was fifteen years old.

The last thing my mother said to me was "Bonnie, would you go for me? I can not do my mission work anymore." Her little part for Jesus was to get the church papers, wrap them up, and mail them to her family.

I replied, "Yes, Mama I can go." I had no idea what God could do with me at thirty-four years old.

After driving a big bus for six years, I had a deep longing to do more for the Lord, who had done so much for me. I was sitting in my school bus one day, praying and asking God what He wanted to do with my life. I said, "Lord, take me where You can use me. Please put me somewhere with children who need me —children I can help."

In 1973, the Portland Public Schools bought another company's special education vans. My boss, Ben, whom I was working with was planning to transfer. I had experience driving a bus with children now, so I could bid on one of the new routes. The route would be closer to home and the bus was smaller, but I wasn't sure I wanted to transfer. Then I realized these were slow-learning kids, just like I had been. I felt the Lord wanted me to drive such a bus and do what I could to help these children. I put in my bid driving a special ed bus for the coming year, and received it.

That fall, as I stepped into my little bus, I knew this was where God wanted me to be. It felt similar to the first time I sat in my big bus. I belonged here with these children. I understood how they felt, and with God's help, I could help them.

After driving the special education bus for several years, the Lord spoke to my heart. "You have been driving this bus for years, and never said a word to these children about bringing them to Sunday school." Oh, how ashamed I felt! I asked God to forgive me for missing so many opportunities. I was determined to begin reaching out to the many children I saw every day.

I walked to my Volkswagen bus, laid my hands on it, and declared, "Lord, fill it up." I contacted the children's parents, and the next Sunday I had sixteen children in that bus for Sunday school. I could hardly get the door closed. We laughed and sang all the way to Sunday school. Oh, how the Lord blessed! And how He multiplied. Our Sunday school not only picked up the children from my bus run, but also their cousins, friends, and neighbors. The number grew until there were over five hundred, and I stopped counting. God did multiply. Truly there is nothing impossible with Him.

The children and I had wonderful times together. I realized some of them were from broken homes like I was and did not know how to read. I brought them home and taught them. We went on picnics, bike rides, and even traveled to the mountains. At that point, I knew why I had gone through so much growing up. God had been preparing me to love these children and tell them, "I understand. I care. I've been there." I had the privilege of saying, "You are going to make it. You can do it. I believe in you and have confidence in you."

Me with some of the children I brought to Sunday school

Just before the Lord gave me all these children, I was reading the Bible one day. I opened it to Isaiah 49:20: "Children thou shalt have, after thou hast lost the other." I thought, *Lord, that doesn't pertain to me. I have not lost my child.* Within two years, my son went away to college. After he left, he married and moved away. That verse did come to pass. God gave me all these children. He wanted me to love them and bring them to Him.

I not only had the opportunity to help children on my school bus, but was fortunate to also help those in the prison ministry. One time, the minister asked me if I could go to prisons and Juvenile Home for teenage boys and girls. I did this for twenty-eight years from 1992 to 2020. Many young teenagers that I visited at the Juvenile Home felt no one loved, cared, or understood them. Many came from very abused homes, grew up in a household without a father or mother, or were in foster care. Some had learning disabilities. To this day, I tell them my life story of how God helped me through difficulties of my childhood such as child abuse, dyslexia, peer pressure in school, and rejection because of my learning disabilities. I give my testimony of how God healed me of cancer, and how He has blessed my life since I gave my heart to Him. God taught me to read and helped me to obtain a wonderful job that I loved, driving a school bus for twenty-six years. God has supplied all my needs and constantly answers my prayers. I truly thank God and praise Him for all His many blessings.

12

GOD PLANNED
MY AWARDS

Ben, my bus-driving manager, always treated his drivers in a gentle, easy-going manner. All of us liked him and got along well together. In 1978, eleven years later, Ben left for another position. A man by the name of Ray took his place. Ray worked under rigid rules and began treating the drivers the same way. I became very unhappy and began harboring a bad view of him. Loving God as I did, I prayed about this. I asked the Lord to forgive me. He did, and showed me I needed to ask Ray to forgive me, also. It wasn't easy, but I approached Ray. "I've been having a bad attitude toward you. I haven't liked your strictness over us drivers. I was wrong to feel that way, and I ask your forgiveness." Ray readily forgave me, and God gave me favor with him.

At that time, a number of organizations (Oregon Pupil Transportation Association, Pioneer News, Bronze Eagle Awards for drivers with special circumstances) were granting awards to deserving drivers—drivers having outstanding safety records, drivers showing extra courtesy on the road, and so on. Transportation supervisors nominated bus drivers for such honors, then the organizations studied the qualifications of nominees and presented the awards. Ray, as a supervisor over my district of Portland Public School Transportations, made a study of the performance of his drivers. Here is the list of qualifications he followed, along with his rating of the driver he nominated:

1. A good job record (Bonnie Davis has driven for 22 years).
2. A good attendance record (Bonnie has had no unexcused absences from work).
3. A good record in past ratings (Bonnie has done safe driving, with no chargeable accidents).
4. An active interest in other worthwhile activities (Bonnie regularly visits shut-ins at senior centers, teaches Sunday school classes, drove a Sunday school bus for nine years, has brought in 500 new Sunday school pupils, shows a loving, caring attitude toward pupils that she transports. She has sometimes taken students to her home and helped them with schoolwork. She has driven them on outings. Often she plays mom to them while they are on her bus—tying their shoes, combing their hair, buttoning their dresses).
5. A good reason for nomination (Bonnie has been an outstanding driver over the years. Many pupils, as well as parents, have expressed appreciation to her for her care and safety over them).

During my years of bus driving under Ray, he nominated me for these three awards, all of which were granted me:

1. 1986 Driver of the Month for Portland Public Schools.
2. 1987-88 Driver of the Year for my school district of Portland Public Schools.
3. 1989-90 Driver of the Year for the state of Oregon.

Me with my 1990 Oregon Driver of the Year Award

Lavelda and I in front of my big bus

In addition to making these nominations, Ray wrote this concise paragraph concerning my "Driver of the Year for the State of Oregon" award:

> Bonnie Davis, a school bus driver for Portland Public Schools, was selected and honored as Oregon School Bus Driver of the Year by the Oregon Pupil Transportation Association at their annual school bus safety exercise in Roseburg, Oregon, on April 28, 1990. Bonnie was once asked, "After your years of piloting buses through traffic, what advice might you give motorists?" Out of her wealth of experience on the road, she gave some suggestions: "I would tell younger drivers to give themselves plenty of

time, so they don't need to be in a hurry. If you have more time you'll keep your mind relaxed and at ease. Also, a tired driver is a poor driver. When you're tired, your mind isn't functioning. Courtesy of the road is important, too. We don't own the road, and we see people all the time who think they do. It's not worth an accident. I'm a Christian. I ask God daily to take care of the children and me and the bus. It's working."

—Adapted from *Oregon Motorist*

Also, here are excerpts adapted from the Portland newspaper, *The Oregonian*, highlighting ways my caring attitude helped award me Oregon Driver of the Year for 1989-90:

Davis does more than just drive young children to school. She also spends time helping students with their homework, taking them on excursions, teaching Sunday school at her church. "Some come to my house and we do crafts," Bonnie said. "Sometimes they help me with my yard work. We've had a lot of fun over the years. Here is one instance: One day as I came to the end of my bus run, I dropped off my last child. Her family came out to invite me into their house. I went in and they had a big surprise birthday party for me." Sometimes when calling on elderly persons at senior centers, Bonnie takes children along to sing and visit. Bonnie would like to have a reunion someday with all the children she has transported on her bus.

After twenty-six years and thousands of miles, God has kept His loving and protecting hand over the children and me. I thank Him for that. Now, I am retired and serving the Lord by traveling and sharing my testimony of what the Lord has done for me. Truly God makes no mistakes. He had a plan for my life.

My manager, Ray, awarding me the 26-year Retirement Award, 1993

13

GOD SAVED MILTON

As time passed and I went about my life, I never forgot my ex-husband. One morning, forty-six years later, I woke up thinking about that night in 1953 and what had happened to me. I started crying. All the pent-up emotions were released from me as I cried for over an hour. Then the Lord gave me a wonderful peace and completely healed my emotions from the damage that had been done to me. God helped me forgive Milton, and I continued to pray for him.

Milton knew about God. He had gone to Sunday school when he was six years old and grew up saying the Lord's Prayer. Twice God had spared his life when he was in the Korean War during 1950 and 1951. The first time, he had been in a foxhole with one of his buddies. The hole was so small that they were standing, shoulder to shoulder, with their arms touching. Bullets flew all around them. A shot went right through his partner and killed him, but Milton wasn't hurt.

In another incident, Milton was on a march with his unit. They did these marches often, carrying heavy machine guns on their backs for miles and miles until they developed blisters on their feet. Sometimes the stabbing pain in his side became so intense he put his gun down. Knowing Milton couldn't go any further, his officers sent him back to base camp. Awfully ill, he was taken to a hospital in Sapporo, Japan where they performed a hernia operation. While in the hospital, his colleagues were sent to the front lines where the enemy took fire, killing most everyone. It was only by the mercy of God Milton was spared.

One morning in 1978, I woke up with Ezekiel 33:8-9 in mind. It reads, "When I say unto the wicked, O wicked man, thou shalt surely die; if thou dost not speak to warn the wicked from his way, that wicked man shall die in his iniquity; but his blood will I require at thine hand. Nevertheless, if thou warn the wicked of his way to turn from it; if he does not turn from his way, he shall die in his iniquity; but thou hast delivered thy soul." I knew this scripture was concerning Milton. I told the Lord I couldn't speak to him about the gospel, but if He put other people in Milton's path to talk to him, I would pray. The Lord promised me, "If you are faithful to pray for him, I will save him."

In 1979, a brother from my church, Dick, told me he had met my ex-husband. He rode two hours to and from work with him, for two months, without knowing who he was. One day, for no reason, Milton said to Dick, "I dislike that ex-wife of mine. She is such a fanatic. That church that she goes to, I'd like to burn it to the ground." Dick asked him which church it was. Milton answered, "The Apostolic Faith Church on 52nd and Duke Street," to which Dick replied, "That's my church, and if you burn it to the ground, I'll come looking for you." Total silence filled the truck after that day. They continued to work together for several months and became good friends despite Dick's affiliation with the aggrieved church. In 1988, I prayed for the two of them to work together again, and God answered that prayer on a different project.

In May 1979, Milton's family planned a big birthday party for his mother, Grandma Davis. They invited everyone she knew. My mail carrier, Allan, happened to be a good friend of hers and was invited to the party. Allan had given his heart to the Lord a year before and was attending my church. When he came with the mail one morning, about three days before the party, I told him, "I believe God wants you to go to Grandma Davis' birthday party and talk to Milton about his soul." He told me he would go if he got off work early.

The party was set for two o'clock Saturday, and it would take thirty-five minutes to drive to the house. The next day, Allan spoke to his supervisor. Unfortunately, there was too much mail to deliver Saturday so he had to work the full shift. When I heard this, I started praying, "God, if you want Allan to be at that party, don't let there be any mail on Saturday." Saturday morning at 8:30 a.m., Allan was standing on my front porch.

"Why are you here so early?" I asked, surprised to see him.

"There was hardly any mail today," he replied. He finished my route by noon and was at the party by two.

While there, Allan had an opportunity to speak to Milton. Another prayer was answered.

———⊰❀⊱———

One morning in March 1982, I woke up and the Lord impressed upon me, "You better warn Milton."

"I can't talk to him," I replied. "Send someone spiritual to talk to him about his soul because I can't."

Two weeks later, another brother from my church, Kenny, was called on by Milton to give a bid on his house gutters. As he knocked on the door, God revealed to him, "This is Bonnie Davis' ex-husband." When Milton answered the door, they talked business for a while, and then he offered Kenny a beer. The offer gave Kenny the opportunity to share his testimony. "Before the Lord saved me, I stayed at the tavern until closing every night," explained Kenny. As he continued to share his life story, the Spirit of God witnessed through him. He later told me Milton listened very intently and was receptive to what he was saying. Milton's mother called me shortly after and repeated Kenny's testimony in detail as she had heard it from her son. What an answer to prayer!

In July of that same year, I was putting strawberries in the freezer one evening when the Lord spoke to me three times as plain as if He were standing right next to me. Each time He said, "I'm going to save Milton." I ran to my bedroom and got on my knees and prayed, "Show me if this is from You, Lord. If it's not my own thoughts then give me a witness. Let me stand behind the cross." My eyes were closed, but immediately God's Spirit filled me and I saw a beautiful wooden cross illuminated. It was gray and rough as if someone had taken a knife to it. Three hours later my mail carrier, Allan, called and said he had been praying and received a witness from the Lord for Milton's salvation. This was the witness I had asked for when I was praying earlier.

That same month, I went to bed one night dreaming about Milton, even though I had not been thinking about him beforehand. In the dream, he was standing up against a wall and was very dirty. His face was old and wrinkled, and he had a very rugged look. I was standing in front of him, looking down at my hands. The palms of my hands were open in front of me. In them was a beautiful, glistening white robe, folded over many times. It was soft and light as a feather. I heard Milton's voice.

He called to me, "Bonnie, did you bring me my white garment?"

I looked at him. He was so grimy that I said, "You can't put this on. You have to get clean first."

"May I have it?" he asked. "I'm going home soon."

I walked toward him, and he reached out to take the robe. As he touched the garment, the wrinkles on his face melted away. He became clean, his face turned peaceful, and all of the hardness was gone. Then I saw his right hand picking up five or six objects from the ground and throwing them out into space. Before I knew it, he had disappeared.

I asked, "Oh, God, could I see him just once more?" I looked up and Milton was looking down at me, smiling. Then he vanished. God gave me the meaning of this dream. He told me Milton was up against the wall because he will be in a difficult place in life. I wondered why he appeared so dirty. God revealed to me that Milton needed to get washed in the Blood of the Lamb and be cleaned before putting on the robe. I asked God what the objects were that Milton was throwing. God simply said He was taking care of him, which gave me hope.

———

While picking raspberries on a Wednesday afternoon in 1988, there was a point when I told the Lord, "I'm tired of praying for Milton. I'm just going to quit."

The Lord responded, "Don't give up; we are almost there."

"Lord, if this is from You, give me a witness," I asked.

The following Saturday I picked up an elderly friend, Margie, from the airport. "I have something to tell you," she insisted. The Lord had woken her up in the middle of the night and told her to pray for Milton. As she prayed, the whole room lit up with the Glory of the Lord, and God witnessed to her that Milton would be saved. When I asked her which day the Lord had revealed this to her, she said Wednesday. This was the same day I asked the Lord for a witness while picking berries.

Upon praying for Milton on a Sunday morning, God gave me Ezekiel 11:19-20: "And I will give them one heart, and I will put a new spirit within you; and I will take the stony heart out of their flesh, and will give them an heart of flesh: That they may walk in my statutes, and keep mine ordinances, and do them: and they shall be my people, and I will be their God." I prayed, "Lord, take away his stony heart."

The following week on Easter 1989, Milton was invited to watch his granddaughters perform in a play at a nursing home. If he had known the play was about asking Jesus into your heart he never would have gone, but God was speaking to him. Milton had a tender heart that day.

In May 1994, the Lord asked me, "Would you pray for Milton's healing?"

"But God, he's not sick," I responded. The Lord repeated the question, so I obeyed.

Near the beginning of 1995, I had a dream in which Milton was sitting in our old house, where we lived while we were married. He was sitting in a chair in the kitchen. The house was desolate and demolished. He had a smile on his face. When I woke up I asked God for the meaning of the dream. He stated, "His earthly house will soon be left desolate."

One month later, God spoke to me again saying, "Milton's earthly house will be left desolate."

"God, if this is from You, give me a witness," I asked. The Lord filled me with His Spirit and gave me Matthew 23:38: "Behold, your house is left unto you desolate."

Milton was diagnosed with liver and lung cancer in April 1995. Since God had taken the pain out of the bad memories I had in connection with my ex-husband, I was able to pray for him out of a place of complete compassion. "Don't let him die until he can be saved," I pleaded to God. Shortly after, I called Milton and told him I was praying for him. He was sweet and tender during the conversation and thanked me.

Two months later, a friend named Dan said he had been praying for Milton. He dreamed that all of Milton's family came to me, thanking me for my prayers. In his dream, they said they could see the Spirit of God in me. After I heard about the dream, I asked God to give me favor with Milton's family. This dream came to pass the day of Grandma Davis' funeral, when Milton's family came to me and thanked me for praying with Grandma Davis.

One morning during that same month, I prayed for Milton with a heavy burden. The Lord told me to go out to the garden. It was about 8 a.m. I walked outside when I felt the Lord say, "Look up!" When I did, I saw a cloud in the form of a cross. "I will do that for Milton," the Lord proclaimed. I knew the cloud was a promise that God would answer my prayers.

On a Sunday night in October 1998, my pastor asked, "Have you prayed for God to do something for someone and He hasn't answered for over forty years?" Just before the pastor said "forty," I prayed, "God, if he says forty years, I will know this is from you." I knew this was a confirmation from the Lord as this was how long I had interceded for Milton.

The next morning, I read Revelation 7:13-14: "And one of the elders answered, saying unto me, What are these which are arrayed in white robes? and whence came they? And I said unto him, Sir, thou knowest. And he said to me, These are they which came out of great tribulation, and have washed their robes, and made them white in the blood of the Lamb." When I finished reading, God said to me, "I'm still answering your prayers for Milton."

I dreamed again about Milton in July 1999. In my dream, he was in the hospital. I could see him in the hospital bed. A woman sat in a chair beside him, with her head down. She sat without saying a word and appeared to be praying. Milton was lying on his left side. A man in a white robe stood by his bed and held out his hand to Milton. They were talking, and Milton was smiling. Milton began to laugh with a holy, joyful laugh, as some people do when they get saved. Then I knew the man was Jesus. Once the man left, Milton passed away. When I awoke, I wasn't sure what the dream meant. I wondered if the woman in the dream was my friend, Vickee, who was a nurse.

Shortly after, God gave me Ezekiel 24:14: "I the Lord have spoken it: it shall come to pass, and I will do it; I will not go back, neither will I spare, neither will I repent; according to thy ways, and according to thy doings, shall they judge thee, saith the Lord God."

Milton's family gathered together for Easter dinner in 2002, and I prayed for an opportunity to speak to Milton alone. When the opportunity presented itself, I asked if he was back on chemotherapy. "Back? I've never been off. Maybe I will live a few more days or months." Toward the end of the evening, as I was about to leave, Milton grabbed my hand and squeezed my fingers hard. He smiled at me. He wanted me to know everything was OK between us, and he appreciated that I was praying for him.

When December came around, I woke up every morning with a heavy burden for Milton and two songs in my mind; "The Comforter Has Come" and "It Is Well With My Soul." It had been nine years since Milton had started chemotherapy for his liver and lung cancer. God was faithful to give him a Christian doctor. The doctor called him "the miracle man." It was unusual for someone with liver and lung cancer to live on chemotherapy for that long. I knew it was God.

In the beginning of the next year, I read in the Bible about Joseph's dreams and how they came to pass. "Let my dreams of Milton in 1982 and 1999 be fulfilled. Please, let me be there when he departs this life," I asked God. The next day I woke up singing, "The Comforter Has Come." Tears ran down my face as I laid in bed singing. Oh, the peace that Jesus gave me! It was wonderful.

On May 18, 2004, I prayed, "Lord, I just give Milton to You. I don't know how to pray for him anymore." One week later, my son called and said his dad couldn't walk anymore. The cancer had spread into his bones.

Later that month, on May 30, Michael called again and said his dad had been admitted into the hospital. "You need to go talk to your dad. Eternity is a long time," I told him.

"Yes, I know; pray for me," Michael responded.

On June 1, I was at home praying in my bedroom for Milton, asking the Lord to save him. All I could say was, "Help Milton to pray. Send someone to pray with him." I did not know this was the day Michael was speaking to him. At 10:30 a.m., God gave me peace. At this same time, Michael was leaving the hospital after praying with his dad. He said he had walked to his dad's bedside, took his face in his hands and said, "I love you." Then Michael looked him in the eyes and said, "I want to meet you in heaven. Would you pray and ask Jesus into your heart?" to which Milton replied, "Yes, I've been praying." Michael asked if he wanted to repeat the sinner's prayer after him. Milton said he did and repeated every word. As Michael prayed, he felt the Spirit of God come over him.

The next day I went to Safeway to buy flowers for Milton. They were sold out, which was very unusual, so I returned home. The following day, I went back again. The Lord impressed upon me, "Buy him something nice." I asked the clerk for a special gift. She brought out three beautiful, rich, full, crimson red rosebuds. These buds were about four inches high, and at the stem about three inches across. They could fit fully in the open palm of my hand. I had never seen anything like them. They were very large, with crimson red velvet on the outside and beautiful pink velvet on the inside. The clerk added a big red bow. They were just perfect, as Milton's favorite color was red and his favorite flower was roses. Later, I wondered why these roses were different from any I had ever seen, so I returned to Safeway and asked. The clerk said Safeway had received a small shipment of them from Brazil, but had not received any since.

As I laid the roses on the car seat next to me and prepared to drive to the hospital, I realized this would have been our fifty-first wedding anniversary. When I got to the hospital, I gave the roses to the staff to deliver and received many compliments on them. Two hours after Milton received the flowers, he was sent home. His current wife called to say that she, too, had never seen anything like those roses. Twice Michael visited his father at home. Milton was never one to give compliments, but twice he said to our son with emotion in his voice, "Do you see those beautiful roses? They are from your mother." When I heard this I knew God had saved him and changed his heart.

On June 15, 2004, the Lord gave me 2 Peter 3:9: "The Lord is not slack concerning his promise, as some men count slackness; but is longsuffering to us-ward, not willing that any should perish, but that all should come to repentance." While I was praying that day, I felt the Lord say, "Call your son." I did, and my daughter-in-law answered the phone. While we were talking, she mentioned Milton was back in the hospital, with only a few hours left to live. I shortened the conversation and hung up the phone.

I wanted to see Milton before he died, but as his ex-wife, I didn't know if I would be welcome in his hospital room. I prayed, "Lord, let me be there when Milton dies." I called my church and asked them to pray that Milton would live long enough for me to get to the hospital, and that I would be able to go into his room.

I arrived at the hospital at 11:30 a.m. I hugged Milton's wife, his sister, and our son. God answered both of my prayers, and I sat down in the chair next to his bed. I began to pray quietly for Milton. Twice, the Spirit of the Lord lifted me up. I stood and laid my hands on his shoulder and prayed, "Jesus, Jesus, Jesus." Nobody stopped me. He recognized my voice and tried to open his eyes, but he couldn't open them all the way.

Later, when I asked his sister if he had opened his eyes before this, she said he hadn't. I sat back down in my chair and continued praying. There was such peace surrounding him. A few minutes later, he passed away. God had answered both of my prayers. Milton lived exactly one hour after I arrived. As he took his last breath, I held out my arms saying, "Can you feel the peace? Oh, the peace." Then I realized this was the dream I had in 1999. I was the woman sitting in the chair next to his bed when he died. Before I left the hospital that day, Milton's wife told me his roses had died that morning. Then I knew God had prepared those roses especially for Milton.

That night I prayed to the Lord, "I believe Milton was saved when he died because I felt the peace surrounding him. Can You give me a verse, so I can be sure?" The Lord did, giving me 2 Peter 3:9 again: "The Lord is not slack concerning his promise, as some men count slackness; but is longsuffering to us-ward, not willing that any should perish, but that all should come to repentance."

The next day I asked God, "Was that verse really from You?" I let my Bible fall open, and it fell to that same verse. When I looked at the page I saw that I had written there, "A promise for Milton, September 5, 1999."

Milton's current wife and my son held a beautiful memorial service for him. The pastor spoke on John 14:2-3: "In my Father's house are many mansions: if it were not so, I would have told you. I go to prepare a place for you. And if I go and prepare a place for you, I will come again, and receive you unto myself; that where I am, there ye may be also." I know that I will see Milton in heaven. Thank You, Lord, for answering my prayers.

My Family

With my precious granddaughters, Allison and Andrea

Lavelda, Vollie, and I

My son, Michael, and I

Left to Right: Me, Jack, Parker, Grayson, and Hudson

Michael, Grayson, Becky, Esmé, Allison, Andrea, Hudson, and I

Esmé and I during Christmas

3-year-old Esmé

(First Row) Andrea, Parker, Jack, Grayson, Hudson
(Back Row) Jason, Becky, Michael, Allison, Esmé, and David

Epilogue

God has been there for me every instance of my life. He has never failed me. He's my all in all, my healer, my counselor, my strength. I praise Him for what He has done in my life. I thank Him for the opportunity He has given me to share how real Jesus is in my life through this book. I have since been able to share my testimony through prison ministry and mission work.

Something Beautiful Hymn
1971 William J. Gaither

Som-thing beau-ti-ful, some-thing
good; All my con-fu-sion
He un-der-stood. All I had to of-fer Him
was bro-ken-ness and strife,
But He made some-thing beau-ti-ful of my life.

Printed in the United States
by Baker & Taylor Publisher Services